The Arctic

by Katherine Scraper

I need to know these words.

fur

fuzz

globe

moss

oil

snow

Look at a **globe**. Find the top
of the globe. You are looking
at the Arctic!

North Pole

the Arctic

▲ The North Pole is in the Arctic.

The Arctic is very cold. The Arctic has **snow** and ice. The Arctic is windy, too.

▲ The temperature in the Arctic can be −30 degrees Fahrenheit (−34 degrees Celsius).

How can animals live in the Arctic? Some animals have fat to keep warm. Some animals have **fur** to keep warm.

◄ A walrus has fat.

▲ A wolf has fur.

Some animals have fat and fur!

▲ A polar bear has fat and fur.

Some animals change colors
to hide. The animals hide
on the snow. The animals hide
on the ground.

The Arctic fox has ▶
gray fur in summer.

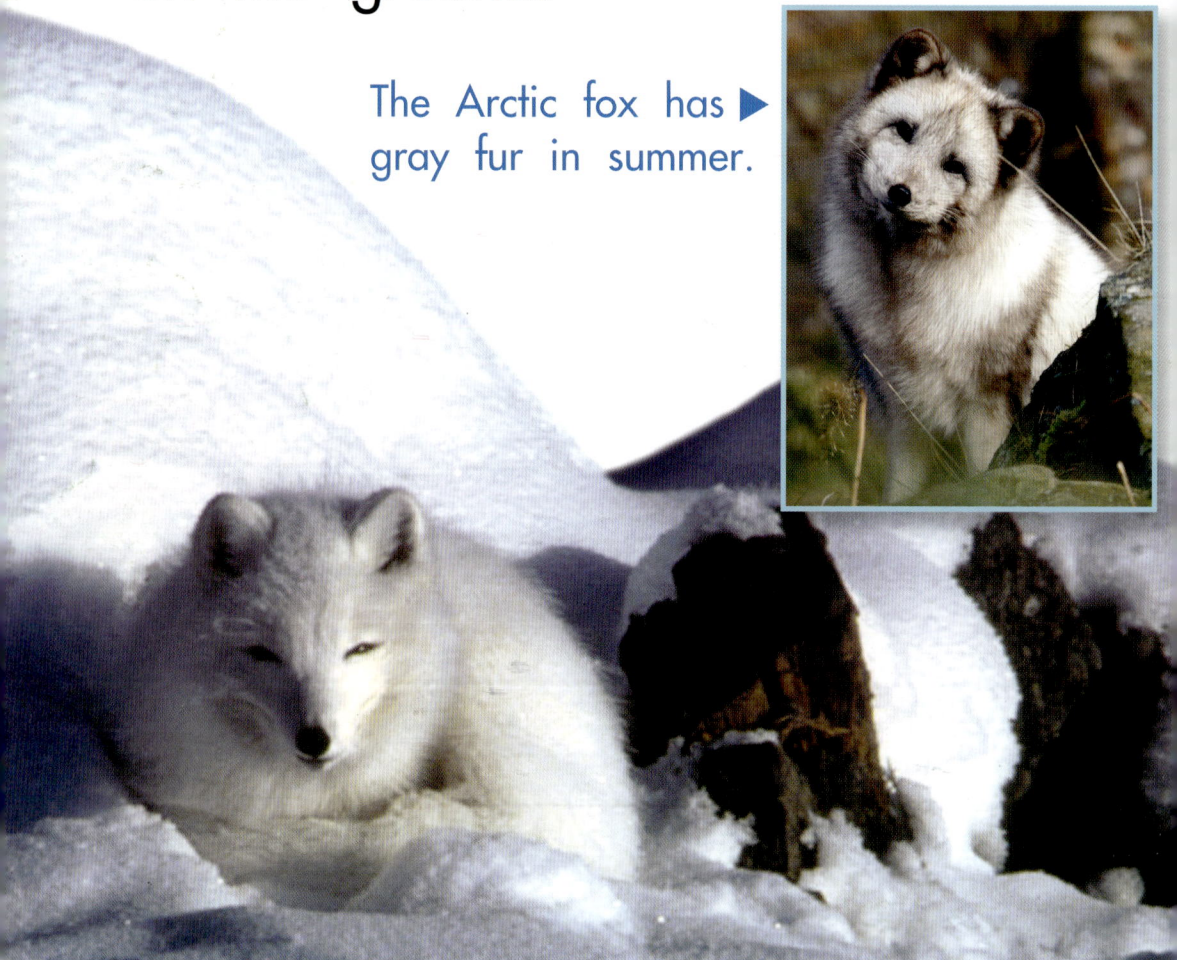

▲ The Arctic fox has white fur in winter.

Some animals go to different places to find food.

▲ This moose lives in the Arctic.

How can plants live in the Arctic? Some flowers look like cups. The cups hold heat from the sun.

▲ The flower on this poppy looks like a cup.

Some plants have **fuzz**. The fuzz helps keep the plant warm. The fuzz keeps wind away from the plant.

▲ This willow has fuzz on the stems and leaves.

Some plants live on rocks. **Moss** can live on rocks.

▲ Moss has very small leaves.
Moss does not have flowers.

Some birds eat moss. Some birds put moss in their nests, too.

▲ The moss helps keep the eggs warm.

The weather can change the Arctic. Warm weather can change snow and ice. The snow and ice can change to water.

▲ Plants and animals must change when the weather changes.

The Arctic has **oil**. People use the oil. The land in the Arctic can change when people take oil.

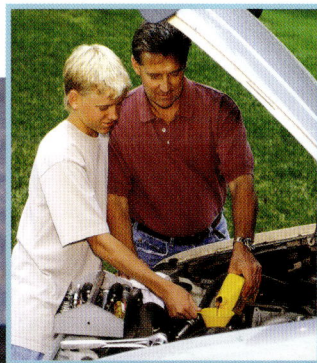

▲ These animals may not find all the food they need.

Plants and animals live in the Arctic!